S0-DFJ-612
Lake Oswego, OR

Language Readers

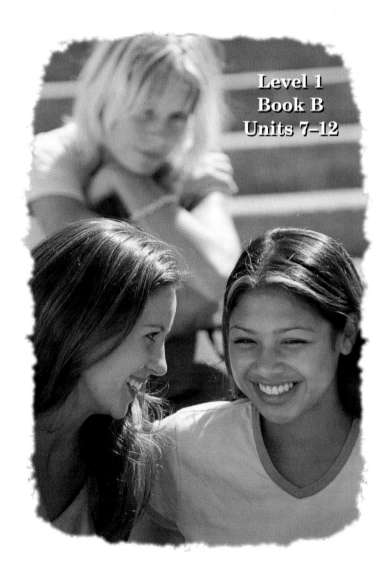

Level 1
Book B
Units 7–12

Jane Fell Greene
Judy Fell Woods

Copyright 2000 (Third Edition) by Jane Fell Greene and Judy Fell Woods.
All rights reserved.

04   03   02   01   00   5   4   3   2   1

ISBN 1-57035-275-5

No portion of this work may be reproduced or transmitted in any form or
by any means, electronic or mechanical, including photocopying or re-
cording, or by any information storage and retrieval system, without the
express written permission of the publisher.

Text layout and design by Kimberly Harris
Cover design by Becky Malone
Cover Image © 2000 by Digital Vision Ltd.
Illustrated by Peggy Ranson

This product is in compliance with AB2519 California State
Adoption revision requirements.

Printed in the United States of America

Published and Distributed by

Sopris West
*Helping You Meet the Needs
of At-Risk Students*

4093 Specialty Place • Longmont, CO 80504 • (303) 651-2829
www.sopriswest.com

Contents

THE RAT PACK

UNIT 7

Phonology/Orthography Concepts

- A single unit of sound is a phoneme.
  - Consonant phonemes are closed sounds.
  - Consonant sound-symbol relationships: **qu**, **x**, **y**, **z**
    qu sounds like /kw/
    x sounds like /ks/
    sometimes **s** sounds like /z/
  - Vowel phonemes are open sounds.
- Combined phonemes (sounds) create words we hear.
- Letters are graphemes (symbols) that represent sounds.
- Combined letters create words we write and read.

Vocabulary

and	quit	yaps
fix	quiz	yips
if	Rat Pack	zaps
Max	sax	zig-zag
mix	six	
quick	yams	

THE RAT PACK

Story Summary:

The kids are fans of a rock group called the Rat Pack. The three rock stars in the group are Mack, Mick, and Rick. Nick's dad takes the whole gang to see the Rat Pack's concert. They are all excited and have a wonderful time. The concert is a big hit with all the pals.

Mack is in the Rat Pack. Mick is in the Rat Pack. Rick is in the Rat Pack.

The Rat Pack is rad! Mack has a hip sax.

Mick can pick it! Rick can zap it! Mack can rap!

The Rat Pack had a gig. The six pals can fit in Nick's dad's van.

"Quick, pack the van, Nick," said Dad. "Fit Pat, Tam, Al, Kim, and Sam in the van."

"Sit in back, Sam. Sit in back, kids." The six kids yip and yap in the back. The van zig-zags.

Nick ran in to the gig. Pat, Tam, Al, Kim, and Sam ran in to the gig.

Nick can rap to the Rat Pack: "Pick it, Mick! Zap it, Rick! Mix it, Mack!"

The Rat Pack can jam. Mick picks it. Rick zaps it. Mack hits it.

"Mix it, Mick! Wax the sax, Mack!"

"I can dig it," said Nick. "It is a kick! It is a hit! The Rat Pack is rad!"

Teacher/Parent Pages

Use the following questions to stimulate language growth, imagination, conceptual relationships, and higher-level thinking skills. These activities will encourage conversation and help develop language skills. Students must know that their ideas are important and that their questions will be heard. Have fun and accept all reasonable answers while praising and encouraging questioning from the students.

Vocabulary Expansion

Describe and define these words and phrases:

rock and roll	concert	dig it
rock group	gig	rad
fan	big hit	hip
superstar	excited	zap it
performance	wax the sax	jam

Language Expansion Activities

1. Act out the story with your friends. Take turns being the Rat Pack and the fans.

2. Get up and dance to some fast music. Make up some new dances and explain to your friends how to do them.

Language Expansion Questions

1. What was the name of the rock group that the kids wanted to go to see?

2. What kids went to the concert? Make a list of their names.

3. How many rock stars were in the Rat Pack? What were their names?

4. How did the kids get to the concert?

5. How did the kids feel when they were at the concert? How do you know?

6. What things did Nick yell to the group as they were playing? Look back in the text to find out if you don't remember.

7. Imagine that you and your friends are superstars. What do you suppose superstars do when they're not performing?

8. Do you think your parents would ever let you go to a rock concert? Would you like to go? Why?

9. Many kids have favorite rock stars. Do you have a favorite? What group or star do you like best? Why?

10. Rock stars have to practice every day. Do you suppose that you could ever practice anything every day? What things would you like to learn how to do better? List them.

MAX ZAPS THE CAN

UNIT 7

Phonology/Orthography Concepts

- A single unit of sound is a phoneme.
  - Consonant phonemes are closed sounds.
  - Consonant sound-symbol relationships: **qu**, **x**, **y**, **z**
    qu sounds like /*kw*/
    x sounds like /*ks*/
    sometimes **s** sounds like /*z*/
  - Vowel phonemes are open sounds.
- Combined phonemes (sounds) create words we hear.
- Letters are graphemes (symbols) that represent sounds.
- Combined letters create words we write and read.

Vocabulary

and	quit	yaps
fix	quiz	yips
if	Rat Pack	zaps
Max	sax	zig-zag
mix	six	
quick	yams	

MAX ZAPS THE CAN

Story Summary:

Sam's fat cat, whose name is Max, loves to roam around exploring in their neighborhood. One day, Max gets into some old garbage cans and eats some spoiled food, which makes him very sick. Sam scolds Max, helps his cat get well, and feeds him some good cat food mix. Max takes a nap.

Max is the fat cat.
Sam is his kid.

The fat cat is
quick. It can zip
and zap.

Max can tip
a big, tin can.

Bam! The tin
can has gas,
yams, tin lids,
bad ham, and
a sad lid.

Max can lick the
can.

"Max! Max! Bad
cat. Quit it!" said
Sam.

Max is sick.
The tin can had
bad ham and
yams.

Max has to lick
his pads.

Sam can fix a
bit of a mix.
Max can have
the mix.

"Lap the mix, Max," said Sam, "lick it."

Max can lap the mix. It is his mix. The mix can fix Max.

Teacher/Parent Pages

Use the following questions to stimulate language growth, imagination, conceptual relationships, and higher-level thinking skills. These activities will encourage conversation and help develop language skills. Students must know that their ideas are important and that their questions will be heard. Have fun and accept all reasonable answers while praising and encouraging questioning from the students.

Vocabulary Expansion

Describe and define these words and phrases:

roam	scold	tin can
neighborhood	zip and zap	curious point of
explore	quit it	view
garbage	mix	knock down
spoiled food	lap	smelly

Language Expansion Activities

1. Draw a picture of the smelly garbage can that Max turned over and licked. Describe how it smelled.

2. Cats are naturally curious. Describe a cat you know. Tell how a cat's curiosity can sometimes get it into trouble.

Language Expansion Questions

1. What was the fat cat's name?

2. Who were the people in Max's family?

3. What happened to Max when he was roaming around the neighborhood?

4. Make a list of all the smelly things that were in the garbage can that Max knocked down.

5. How did Max feel after he ate the spoiled food? How do you know?

6. What did Sam do to help Max feel better?

7. Suppose Max was your cat. What things could you have done to help Max feel better? List them.

8. Retell the story from Max's point of view.

9. Do you have a pet? Tell about it. If you don't have a pet, would you like to? Why or why not?

10. Decide whether Max was treated fairly for what he had done.

THE QUICK FIX

UNIT 7

Phonology/Orthography Concepts

- A single unit of sound is a phoneme.
  - Consonant phonemes are closed sounds.
  - Consonant sound-symbol relationships: **qu**, **x**, **y**, **z**
    qu sounds like /kw/
    x sounds like /ks/
    sometimes **s** sounds like /z/
  - Vowel phonemes are open sounds.
- Combined phonemes (sounds) create words we hear.
- Letters are graphemes (symbols) that represent sounds.
- Combined letters create words we write and read.

Vocabulary

and	quit	yaps
fix	quiz	yips
if	Rat Pack	zaps
Max	sax	zig-zag
mix	six	
quick	yams	

THE QUICK FIX

Story Summary:

Sam's dad is driving him to his baseball game in their new van. The van stops running and Dad becomes irritated. Sam is supposed to be there at six o'clock. Sam gets out a repair kit that is stored in back. Dad discovers that they had a defective gas cap and had lost their fuel. He makes the necessary repairs and adds gas from a gas can. They are back on the road and on their way to Sam's game.

Dad is mad.
His van has quit.

"Fix it, Dad,"
Sam said. "Fix it!
Quick! I have to
bat at six."

"I have six tin
pins in the van kit,"
said Dad.

Dad can fit the six
tin pins in back of
the rim of the van.

"The gas cap
is bad, Dad,"
said Sam.

"I can rig it
back in to the
rim," Dad said to
Sam.
The van had a
quick fix.

"It has gas," Dad said to Sam.

"Sit, Sam. Sit in back. Is Max in the van?" said Dad.
   Max hid in back.

"Max! Max!" Sam said. "Dad can fix the van quick."

Dad sat. Max, the cat, is in the van. Sam is in the van.

The van zig-zags. Max yips and yaps. It is six. Sam is sad and Dad is mad.

Teacher/Parent Pages

Use the following questions to stimulate language growth, imagination, conceptual relationships, and higher-level thinking skills. These activities will encourage conversation and help develop language skills. Students must know that their ideas are important and that their questions will be heard. Have fun and accept all reasonable answers while praising and encouraging questioning from the students.

Vocabulary Expansion

Describe and define these words and phrases:

baseball	teammates	discover
Little League	repair kit	rig it
stall	defective	quick fix
irritated	fuel	frustrated
on time	gas can	trunk

Language Expansion Activities

1. Make the noise the van made when it stalled.

2. Pantomime fixing a car. See if your friend can describe what you are doing to the car as you pretend to fix it.

Language Expansion Questions

1. Where was Sam going when the story began?

2. What time was Sam supposed to be at the game? Why was it important for Sam to be on time for the game?

3. What happened to Dad's van?

4. How did Dad fix the van? Do you think the van was really fixed or that it would need further work? Why?

5. At the end of the story, Sam was sad and Dad was mad. Why were they feeling that way?

6. Dad told Sam to get the repair kit out of the trunk. Do you have a repair kit in your trunk? Make a list of tools that might be in an auto repair kit.

7. Have you ever been in a car when it stopped running? Tell about it.

8. Sam was upset because he wanted to be at the game on time. Have you ever been late for an event when it wasn't your fault? Did you feel frustrated? Write or tell about it.

9. How would the story have been different if Sam's dad's van hadn't stalled? Would the story have been as interesting? Why?

10. Describe how Sam's teammates felt when Sam arrived late for the game.

TAM'S DOG, TAB

UNIT 8

Phonology/Orthography Concepts

- A single unit of sound is a phoneme.
  - Vowel phonemes are open sounds.
  - Combined sounds create words we hear.
- Letters are symbols that represent sounds.
  - Combined letters create words we write and read.
  - Vowel sound-symbol relationship: short **o**
- Nonphonetic words are words that are not spelled (encoded) as they sound.

Vocabulary

Bob	lock	sock	*was*
box	lot	taxi	
cot	Mom	tick-tock	
dock	nod	Tom	
dog	not	top	
dot	pop	tot	
hot	Pop		
job	rock		

TAM'S DOG,
TAB

Story Summary:

Sam is practicing tricks on his skateboard. His cat, Max, jumps on the board to take a ride and holds on by biting on Sam's sock. Tab, Tam's dog, sees Max and chases after him. Tam can't find Tab and she gets a little worried. When she discovers that Tab has chased Max, she scolds Tab for running off. Sam comes by and shares a cold drink with Tam.

Sam can hop
and zig-zag and
pop. Max bit on
Sam's sock.
"Quick, Max,
hop on," said Sam.

Tam's dog, Tab,
sat. Tab was a hot
dog. It was hot.

Tab sat on top
of his cot.

Tab yips and yaps.
Did Tab have a pal?

Tab ran back to
Sam and Max.
Can Tab lick
Max? The dog
ran at Sam and
Max.

Tam said, "Tab
is not on the
cot."

Tam sat and said, "Tab, Tab, quit it, Tab! I am mad. Max is a cat. It is bad to zap a cat."

Tab ran back to Tam and got on his cot. Tam and Tab sat on his cot.

Tam said, "Bad dog. Quit it. Sit on the cot."

Tab sits. Tab licks Tam. Tam pats the dog.

Sam nods to Tam. "Tab is not a bad dog," said Sam.

Sam, Max, Tab, and Tam sat on the cot. Tam said to Sam, "Mom has a lot of pop. Sip a can of pop, Sam."

Teacher/Parent Pages

Use the following questions to stimulate language growth, imagination, conceptual relationships, and higher-level thinking skills. These activities will encourage conversation and help develop language skills. Students must know that their ideas are important and that their questions will be heard. Have fun and accept all reasonable answers while praising and encouraging questioning from the students.

Vocabulary Expansion

Describe and define these words and phrases:

practice	run off	a hot dog
skateboard	tricks	pop a wheelie
chase	share	taxicab
worry	jump on	quit it
scold	hold on	zap it

Language Expansion Activities

1. Describe all of the skateboard tricks you have seen people do or you have seen on TV. Draw a picture of each one, and print the names of the tricks under the pictures.

2. In the library, find information about a special kind of dog or cat you like. Then give a report to your group.

Language Expansion Questions

1. Explain what was meant in the story by, "Sam can hop and zig-zag and pop."

2. Why did Max bite on Sam's sock?

3. Describe the weather on the day of this story.

4. How do you think Tam felt about her dog, Tab, chasing Sam's fat cat, Max?

5. Do you think that Max could take care of himself? Why do you think so?

6. How do most cats behave when they are chased by dogs? Are there any special abilities cats have to protect themselves?

7. Why was Tam worried?

8. Is it fair to be angry with a dog for behaving the way dogs behave? Can we expect dogs to behave like people?

9. What kinds of responsibilities do pet owners have? List them.

10. If you could select any pet in the world, what pet would you select? Explain why.

POP HAS A NAP

UNIT 8

Phonology/Orthography Concepts

- A single unit of sound is a phoneme.
  - Vowel phonemes are open sounds.
  - Combined sounds create words we hear.
- Letters are symbols that represent sounds.
  - Combined letters create words we write and read.
  - Vowel sound-symbol relationship: short **o**
- Nonphonetic words are words that are not spelled (encoded) as they sound.

Vocabulary

Bob	lock	sock	*was*
box	lot	taxi	
cot	Mom	tick-tock	
dock	nod	Tom	
dog	not	top	
dot	pop	tot	
hot	Pop		
job	rock		

POP HAS A NAP

Story Summary:

While his dad and cat are napping, Sam and his pal, Tom, have a noisy spat. Dad and the cat are awakened. Dad rouses Tom, who has been knocked down, and admonishes Sam. Dad then encourages the boys to make up and play quietly. The boys have a snack. Both Dad and the cat return to their afternoon snooze.

Sam's pop is not at his job. Pop is hot. Pop has a quick nap.

A fat cat's job is to nap. Max, Sam's fat cat, can nap a lot!

Sam has a pal, Tom. Sam is mad at Tom. Tom picks on Max.

Sam ran at Tom.
Tom said, "Max
is a bad cat."
Sam said, "Tom,
quit it. Max is
not bad. Quit it."

Tom hits Sam.
Sam can box
Tom.

Bam! Pow! Bop!
Zap! Zip! It is bad
if Sam pops Tom
and Tom bops
Sam.

Tom got hit.
Pop fans him.

Pop nabs Sam.
Pop said, "Sam,
Tom was hit." Pop
was hot!

Sam said, "I
am not mad,
Tom."
Tom said, "I
am not mad,
Sam."

Tom is
Sam's pal.
Sam is
Tom's pal.
Tom and
Sam have hot dogs and pop.

 Pop and
Max have a
bit of a nap.

Teacher/Parent Pages

Use the following questions to stimulate language growth, imagination, conceptual relationships, and higher-level thinking skills. These activities will encourage conversation and help develop language skills. Students must know that their ideas are important and that their questions will be heard. Have fun and accept all reasonable answers while praising and encouraging questioning from the students.

Vocabulary Expansion

Describe and define these words and phrases:

snooze	friend	make up
catnap	fight	snack
doze	spat	rest
quarrel	pass out	weekend
chum	shake hands	quiet

Language Expansion Activities

1. Tell a story about you and your pal making up after a quarrel. Explain why friends sometimes fight.

2. Act out another way that Sam and Tom could have resolved their differences.

Language Expansion Questions

1. What were Dad and the cat trying to do?

2. What happened to awaken Dad and the fat cat?

3. What did Tom say about Max?

4. Why did Sam run at his pal and start a fight?

5. Explain how Dad helped the pals solve their problem.

6. How do you think Dad felt when he had to break up the fight?

7. How would you help your pals break up a fight?

8. Identify an event in the story that has happened to you. Write about it.

9. Choose one pal from the story to be your friend. Who would you choose? Why?

10. Why do people take naps? Why do they sleep at night?

11. In the story, Sam and Tom had a snack. What kinds of snacks do you like? Make a list of your favorite snacks.

A POP ON
A DOCK

UNIT 8

Phonology/Orthography Concepts

- A single unit of sound is a phoneme.
  - Vowel phonemes are open sounds.
  - Combined sounds create words we hear.
- Letters are symbols that represent sounds.
  - Combined letters create words we write and read.
  - Vowel sound-symbol relationship: short **o**
- Nonphonetic words are words that are not spelled (encoded) as they sound.

Vocabulary

Bob	lock	sock	*was*
box	lot	taxi	
cot	Mom	tick-tock	
dock	nod	Tom	
dog	not	top	
dot	pop	tot	
hot	Pop		
job	rock		

A POP ON A DOCK

Story Summary:

Sam, Tam, Tab, and Max are sitting near a little mall at the dock, waiting for a taxicab. They wait for a long time. When the cab finally arrives, they get in, but they don't get far, because the cab has two flat tires. As soon as repairs are made, they all get back in the cab and take off.

Sam was on the dock.

Max hops on top of the dock. Max licks his lips.

Tam sat on the dock.

Tam said, "The taxi cab is not as quick as Max and Tab! Did the taxi cab quit?"

"Yip! Yap!" said Tab.

"The taxi cab!" said Sam and Tam.

Sam and Tam got in the taxi cab. Tab and Max got in the taxi cab.

The taxi cab did not hop. It did not jig. It did not zip.

"The taxi cab sags and lags," said Sam.

Pop! Bam!
Rip! Pop!

The taxi cab
sits on its big
tin rims. It has
to have a quick
fix.

Sam said, "The
taxi cab can zip.
It can hop. It has
had its quick
fix." Sam got in
the taxi cab.

Tam was in the taxi cab. Tam said, "The taxi cab was sick!"

A lot of pals got back in the taxi cab on the dock. The taxi cab had a fix. It can zip off.

Teacher/Parent Pages

Use the following questions to stimulate language growth, imagination, conceptual relationships, and higher-level thinking skills. These activities will encourage conversation and help develop language skills. Students must know that their ideas are important and that their questions will be heard. Have fun and accept all reasonable answers while praising and encouraging questioning from the students.

Vocabulary Expansion

Describe and define these words and phrases:

mall	take off	wheels
finally	break down	tires
flat tire	blow out	rims
repair	dock	taxicab
await	stores	delay

Language Expansion Activities

1. Tell the group about a time you were getting ready to go someplace, but were delayed.

2. Sam and Tam waited for the tires to be repaired. What else could they have done? Make a list of their choices.

Language Expansion Questions

1. Why do you think Sam and Tam were sitting at the dock? What could they have been doing?

2. Sam had Max, and Tam had Tab. Is it possible to take a pet everywhere you go? Explain why.

3. Why didn't the cab driver arrive on time? What could have caused Sam and Tam to have to wait so long?

4. When the cab finally picked them up, it didn't go. Why not?

5. What do you think is meant by this story's title, "A Pop on a Dock"?

6. How do you think the taxicab driver felt about having two flat tires?

7. Why is it important to change a flat tire and not to drive on it?

8. Where do most drivers keep their spare tires? What tools are needed to repair a flat tire? List them.

9. What do you think Tam really meant when she said, "The taxicab was sick!"?

10. What kinds of things can cause flat tires?

MISS PITT

UNIT 9

Phonology/Orthography Concepts

- Place value for encoding:
  - At the ends of one-syllable words, four consonants are doubled: **-ss**, **-ll**, **-ff**, **-zz**

Vocabulary

Bill	lass	quill	*you*
doll	Liz	sill	
hill	Miss	till	
hiss	off	toss	
jazz	pass	will	
Jill	pill		
kiss	Pitt		

MISS PITT

Story Summary:

Miss Pitt's class is working on a map activity. The students have to find places on the map and spot them with a map pin. But the map pins are missing, so nobody can do the task. All of a sudden, the map pins spill out of Nick's backpack. He was trying to hide them because he didn't understand the lesson. The kids laugh. Nick is humiliated.

Miss Pitt is at the map. "Kids, you have to tack pins on the map. I will pick a tag. You can pin it on the map. The map pins are in the box on the sill. Can you do it?" said Miss Pitt.

Kim, Sid, Sam, Pat, and Tam can do it. Nick can not do it.

Nick got the box of map pins off the sill.

"Kim," said Miss Pitt, "can you tack a pin on the map at Quill Pass?"

"I will," said Kim. Kim got to the map.

"Sid," said Miss Pitt, "tack a pin at the big mill on the top of the hill."

Sid said, "I can do it, Miss Pitt."

"Pat," said Miss Pitt, "can you tack a pin at Big Rock Pass?"

"I can," said Pat.

"Is the pin on the map, Kim?" said Miss Pitt.

"The pin is not on the map, Miss Pitt," said Kim. "I do not have a pin."

"Is the pin on the map, Sid?" said Miss Pitt.

"The pin is not on the map, Miss Pitt," said Sid. "I do not have a pin."

"Pat, is the box of pins on the sill at the map?"

"It is not on the sill, Miss Pitt," said Pat.

"Miss Pitt," said a kid in the back, "Nick has the box of pins."

"Nick, the box of pins is not on the sill at the map. Do you have the box of pins?" said Miss Pitt.

"Do I have the box of pins?" said Nick as the box of pins spills on top of his back pack!

"Quick, Nick, pick the box and the pins off the back pack. Pass the box of pins to me," said Miss Pitt.

Teacher/Parent Pages

Use the following questions to stimulate language growth, imagination, conceptual relationships, and higher-level thinking skills. These activities will encourage conversation and help develop language skills. Students must know that their ideas are important and that their questions will be heard. Have fun and accept all reasonable answers while praising and encouraging questioning from the students.

Vocabulary Expansion

Described and define these words and phrases:

Social Studies	steal	unprepared
map skills	realize	lesson
locate	embarrass	student
perform	hide	teacher
disappear	identify	learn

Language Expansion Activities

1. Draw a map of a place you are familiar with. Tell your class about the places on your map.

2. Ask your parents or an adult that you know if you can look at a map that they have. Talk about the places on the map. See if you can learn to locate a place on the map.

Language Expansion Questions

1. What kind of lesson was Miss Pitt giving her class?

2. Did the students seem to enjoy the lesson? Why?

3. Who took the box of map pins? Why?

4. Because Nick took the box of map pins, the rest of the kids had trouble locating the places on the map for their teacher. Do you think Nick was thinking of himself or of others when he took the box of pins?

5. The story doesn't say how Miss Pitt punished Nick for taking the pins. What do you think she did?

6. Sometimes things get very hard for people and they think that they can't do them. When this happens, sometimes people do foolish things. Have you ever tried very hard to do or remember something that you felt you just couldn't do? What did you do about it?

7. Nick decided that learning the places on the map was too hard for him and he thought taking the pins would help, but it didn't. What else could Nick have done to help him learn the places on the map?

8. Decide how the story would have been different if Nick hadn't taken the box of pins.

9. Nick doesn't seem to like map skills. But he is very good in math. Do you have some subjects that you like better than others? What are they? Write about them.

10. What do you think might happen the next time Miss Pitt has a map skills lesson?

BILL AND JILL

UNIT 9

Phonology/Orthography Concepts

- Place value for encoding:
  - At the ends of one-syllable words, four consonants are doubled: **-ss**, **-ll**, **-ff**, **-zz**

Vocabulary

Bill	lass	quill	*you*
doll	Liz	sill	
hill	Miss	till	
hiss	off	toss	
jazz	pass	will	
Jill	pill		
kiss	Pitt		

BILL AND JILL

Story Summary:

Tam is at home baby-sitting for her younger brother and sisters. Her parents and older brother and sister are at work. The twin babies, Bill and Jill, begin to cry. Tam is a good baby-sitter and calms them down. But she would rather be with her friends.

Tam's mom and dad have a lot of kids. Jack and Liz, the big kids, have jobs. Sis is six. Bill is a tot. Jill is a tot.

Tam said, "Mom, Dad, Liz, and Jack have jobs." It is Tam's job to sit Sis, Jill, and Bill.

"Sis, pass the doll to Jill. Jill is sad," said Tam.

Bill is mad. Bill yips and yips.
"Pass him his jack-in-the-box, Sis," said Tam.

Bill will toss the jack-in-the-box at Jill.

Bill and Jill yip and yip. Bill and Jill miss Mom.

"Can I have a kiss, Bill and Jill?" said Tam.

Bill and Jill kiss Tam. Tam rocks Bill and Jill.
"Can I have the doll, Tam?" said Sis.

"You can have the doll," said Tam.

Bill and Jill
have a nap. Sis
has the doll.

Tam sits at
the sill.

Teacher/Parent Pages

Use the following questions to stimulate language growth, imagination, conceptual relationships, and higher-level thinking skills. These activities will encourage conversation and help develop language skills. Students must know that their ideas are important and that their questions will be heard. Have fun and accept all reasonable answers while praising and encouraging questioning from the students.

Vocabulary Expansion

Describe and define these words and phrases:

baby-sit	large family	windowsill
toddler	parents	wistful thinking
twins	fussy	outdoors
sister	overwhelmed	sibling
brother	settle down	jack-in-the-box

Language Expansion Activities

1. Act out the story, taking turns being Tam and her brothers and sisters.

2. Draw a picture of your family. Tell about each member.

Language Expansion Questions

1. Why did Tam have to baby-sit?

2. How many people were in Tam's family? Can you remember their names? Look back in the text to help you remember.

3. How do you think Tam felt about baby-sitting?

4. The twins were hard to manage and Tam felt very frustrated when they started throwing things. How did she settle them down?

5. What happened at the end of the story?

6. Tam has a large family. How many people are in your family?

7. Sometimes it's hard to manage babies. They cry and get fussy a lot. Do you have any babies or toddlers in your family? Are they sometimes hard to manage? How do you feel about babies? Write about your feelings.

8. Bill and Jill are twins. Do you know any twins? Do you think it would be fun to have a twin sister or brother? Do you think there might be any problems with being a twin?

9. Tam did a marvelous job baby-sitting for her siblings. Do you think you would have done as well? What are some things babies and toddlers like to do?

10. At the end of the story, Tam was sitting at the windowsill thinking about how much fun it would be to play with her friends. Have you ever had to stay in the house and do something for your parents instead of going out to play? How did you handle that situation?

WILL AL WIN?

UNIT 9

Phonology/Orthography Concepts

- Place value for encoding:
  - At the ends of one-syllable words, four consonants are doubled: **-ss**, **-ll**, **-ff**, **-zz**

Vocabulary

Bill	lass	quill	*you*
doll	Liz	sill	
hill	Miss	till	
hiss	off	toss	
jazz	pass	will	
Jill	pill		
kiss	Pitt		

WILL AL WIN?

Story Summary:

Al has finished his map quiz, so Miss Pitt lets him play his favorite computer game, "Rats on Hills." Al places a disk in the computer and begins the game. Al loves playing the game and is very skilled at it. He successfully passes each rat at the top of each hill, winning the game. He has to stop playing because Nick, who hasn't finished his map quiz, needs to work on the computer.

Al is the kid at the PC. Al said, "I will sit at the PC till I win."

Al thinks, "I did pass the map quiz. Miss Pitt said I can sit and pick a CD for the PC. I will pick *Rats on Hills*, till I win."

Al fit the CD, *Rats on Hills*, in Miss Pitt's PC.

Al thinks, "This CD has lots of rats. The rats tip rocks off hills and pass kids to win. I can win if I pass six rats on six hills."

Al got the CD in to the PC. A rat was on top of hill #1. The rat said, "Hiss! Hiss!"

Al thinks, "You will miss, rat! I will pass you!"

"I can pass you on top of hill #1," thinks Al. "I can pass you rats. I can win!"

The rat can kick and toss rocks. Can Al pass the rocks and the rat?

The rat ran. Al can pass the rat and the rocks.

Not a lot of kids can pass Rat Six. Al was as quick as the rat.

"I did it! I did it, Miss Pitt! I can pass Rat Six in *Rats on Hills*."

"You did it, Al," said Miss Pitt. "Can Nick sit at the PC?"

Nick did not pass his map quiz. Nick will sit at the PC and pass his map quiz.

Teacher/Parent Pages

Use the following questions to stimulate language growth, imagination, conceptual relationships, and higher-level thinking skills. These activities will encourage conversation and help develop language skills. Students must know that their ideas are important and that their questions will be heard. Have fun and accept all reasonable answers while praising and encouraging questioning from the students.

Vocabulary Expansion

Describe and define these words and phrases:

computer	privilege	skill
computer program	space bar	successful
disk	return	pass
monitor	computer game	finish
disk drive	rules	quiz

Language Expansion Activities

1. If you have a computer in your school, ask your teacher to let you play a computer game on it after you finish your work.

2. Plan a new computer game. What kinds of characters would be in your game? What would be the goal of the game?

Language Expansion Questions

1. Why did Al get to play on the computer?

2. Did Miss Pitt have a good idea about what games kids would like?

3. What did the children have to do before they could choose a computer game?

4. What was the name of Al's game? What was the goal of the game?

5. Why couldn't Nick play the game?

6. Many children like to play computer or video games. Name some games that you like to play.

7. When Al played "Rats on Hills," he won. Do you usually win when you play video games? Why is winning computer games difficult for some children and easy for others?

8. Some kids don't like to play computer games. What are some other kinds of games that those children might like?

9. People get a certain kind of feeling when they win. Can you describe that kind of feeling?

10. Suppose someone in your family suddenly said, "You can have a new computer and I'll give you any game you want to go with it." What game would you choose?

BANG, RING, SING!

UNIT 10

Phonology/Orthography Concepts

- Sound-symbol relationships: **-ng**, **-nk**
- Consonant letter pairs *-ng* and *-nk* are used only at the **ends** of English words.

Vocabulary

bang	long	sink	*what*
ding-dong	pink	song	
gang	ring	tank	
gong	rink	wings	
honk	sang	yank	
king	sing		

BANG, RING, SING!

Story Summary:

Kim's mom is at home in bed because she is sick. She has a fever and is trying to rest. Kim is offering to get her a cold drink when some friends arrive, bang on the door, ring the bell, sing, and make noises. Through the window, Kim asks them to be quiet, but they keep being noisy. Finally, she goes down to the door and tells them they are inconsiderate. They apologize and leave. Kim prepares dinner for her mom and sits at the windowsill, wondering about her friends.

Ding-Dong!
Bang!
"What is it?"

"Did you ring, Kim? Do not ring and bang. I am sick. I am hot," said Mom.

"Can I fix you a can of pop?" Kim said. "You are hot, Mom. You are sick."

A gang of kids rang and rang. The kids sang a song. Bam! Bang! "Kim! Kim!"

"Did you ring, Nick? Did you bang, Sam? Quit it. Do not ring. I can not have you in," said Kim.

"The kids have got to quit," Mom said. "I am sick. I have to have a nap. Will you pass me a pill, Kim?"

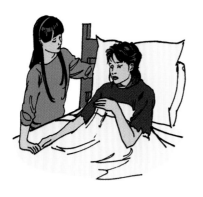

"Nod off, Mom," said Kim.

Kim was mad at the kids. The gang sang and rang. "Kim! Kim! Have you got a song to sing? Can you bang a gong?"

"Quit it!" Kim said. "I am mad at you. Mom is sick and had a pill. I said to quit it. What did you do? Bang, sing, ring."

Kim got a big
tin can. Kim got
the top off the
can. "I will fill

the pan. I can fix it for Mom."

Kim sat
at the sill.
"Mom can
have a nap.
I will have
a can of
pop. What will I miss? The
gang is off." Tick-tock. Is the
pan hot?

Teacher/Parent Pages

Use the following questions to stimulate language growth, imagination, conceptual relationships, and higher-level thinking skills. These activities will encourage conversation and help develop language skills. Students must know that their ideas are important and that their questions will be heard. Have fun and accept all reasonable answers while praising and encouraging questioning from the students.

Vocabulary Expansion

Describe and define these words and phrases:

considerate	fever	cooperate
inconsiderate	chills	assistance
nod off	headache	prepare
apologize	pain	sill
wondering	helpful	rude

Language Expansion Activities

1. Kim's family has two people. Tam's family has many people. How many people are in your family? Draw a big picture of your family and tell everyone in your group about the family members.

2. Think of something you would like to fix your family for dinner. Make a list of all the things you would need to make the meal. Write a list of directions. Be sure to put the steps in order.

Language Expansion Questions

1. Why was Kim trying to be quiet?

2. What was Kim going to get for her mom?

3. What was the cause of all the noise at the front door?

4. Do you think Kim would rather go out and play with her friends or stay inside?

5. Why did Kim stay indoors with her mom?

6. What do you think she was going to make her mom for dinner?

7. Has someone in your family ever been sick? How did you help him or her?

8. Why is it important for people in families to help each other? Discuss the ways that the people in your family help each other.

9. What are some important things to do for people who are sick in bed?

10. At the end of the story, how did Kim feel? How do you think Kim would feel tomorrow if she had gone out to play with her friends?

THE KING
OF THE RINK

UNIT 10

Phonology/Orthography Concepts

- Sound-symbol relationships: **-ng**, **-nk**
- Consonant letter pairs -*ng* and -*nk* are used only at the **ends** of English words.

Vocabulary

bang	long	sink	*what*
ding-dong	pink	song	
gang	ring	tank	
gong	rink	wings	
honk	sang	yank	
king	sing		

THE KING OF THE RINK

Story Summary:

The kids are at the skating rink. The jukebox is playing and they are having fun singing and skating. They soon begin to play a skating game, "King of the Rink." The winner has to grab a ring hanging from a tall rack while skating by. Sid skates along and dreams of winning, but knows that Pat and Sam are the best skaters. All of a sudden, a kid falls down in front of the pack. Many other skaters fall down on top of him. Now it's anybody's game!

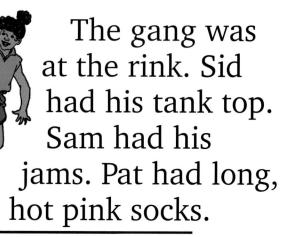

The gang was at the rink. Sid had his tank top. Sam had his jams. Pat had long, hot pink socks.

What song is on the box at the rink? Can the gang sing the song?

The kids pack in to the rink.

Sam can pass
the pack of kids
as if his back had
wings.

Pat is quick. Pat
can zip the laps in
the rink.

The King of the
Rink is the kid to
pass the pack.
　　The king has to
yank the ring off
the rink's top rack.

Zig-zag. Zig-zag. The pack laps and laps.

Sid is not as quick as Sam and Pat. Will Sam and Pat pass Sid?

Sid said, "Can I pass Pat and Sam? Will I yank the ring off the rack? The gong will ring if I am the king."

Bang! Zonk! A lot of kids in the pack got on top of Pat and Sam.

Will Sid pass the pack and yank the ring off the rack? Will the gong ring?

"I did it!" Sid said. "I have the ring! I am the King of the Rink! Ring the gong! I am the king!"

Teacher/Parent Pages

Use the following questions to stimulate language growth, imagination, conceptual relationships, and higher-level thinking skills. These activities will encourage conversation and help develop language skills. Students must know that their ideas are important and that their questions will be heard. Have fun and accept all reasonable answers while praising and encouraging questioning from the students.

Vocabulary Expansion

Describe and define these words and phrases:

jukebox	dream of winning	yank
skating rink	accident	gather
roller skating	results	King of the Rink
ice skating	several	the best
amateur	piling up	the winner

Language Expansion Activities

1. After you read the story, draw pictures of Sid, Sam, and Pat. Pay attention to the way they are dressed. Explain why people dress differently for different activities.

2. If you had a jukebox, what songs would you like it to play? Make a list of the names of the songs.

Language Expansion Questions

1. Where were the kids when this story took place?

2. According to the story, who were the best skaters? Who was the worst skater?

3. What does this mean: "as if his back had wings"?

4. Describe the game the kids called "King of the Rink." What did they have to do to win?

5. Explain some reasons why Sid might not have been as fast as Sam and Pat.

6. Is anybody good at everything? Is anybody bad at everything? Make a list of the things you can do best.

7. Think of something you wish you could do, but that you can't do now. Describe the things you would have to accomplish to really achieve your goal.

8. What happened at the skating rink when someone became King of the Rink? See if you can create the sound of a gong.

9. When the kids started to fall and pile up, where were Pat and Sam? Where was Sid?

10. Pretend that you are Sid. Tell how you felt when you became King of the Rink.

BANG THE GONG

UNIT 10

Phonology/Orthography Concepts

- Sound-symbol relationships: **-ng**, **-nk**
- Consonant letter pairs *-ng* and *-nk* are used only at the **ends** of English words.

Vocabulary

bang	long	sink	*what*
ding-dong	pink	song	
gang	ring	tank	
gong	rink	wings	
honk	sang	yank	
king	sing		

BANG THE GONG

Story Summary:

The students in Miss Pitt's class are putting on a talent show for their families. Miss Pitt will bang a gong when the winner is selected. Each act is different and each child performs well. At the end of the show, Miss Pitt has to bang the gong for all the students, because each performance was excellent.

Moms, dads, and kids are at the big hit. Will Miss Pitt's kids have a hit?

The kids can sing, tap, kick, hiss, and zap.

Kim will sing a long song. Kim's song is a sad song. Kim can sing "The Lass Longs to Kiss the Lad."

114

Tam and Pat tap. The tap has bops, kicks, hops, and jigs. Pat and Tam pass and toss the rods. The tap is hot. Pat and Tam can not miss.

 Sis said, "Tam and Pat will win!" Moms, dads, and kids dig it!

Sid locks Sam in a big tin box. "Zip! Zap!" said Sid. Sam is not in the box. Did Sid zap Sam?

Sam's mom said, "Sam! Sam!" Sam is back in the box!

Nick has got his sax. His song is hot jazz. Nick is a hit!

Al has Bob, an odd doll. Bob sits on Al's lap. Bob said, "What is as fat as a pig?" Al said, "I do not have it, Bob." "A cat in a big, pink box!" said Bob.

"Hiss! Hiss!" said moms, dads, and kids.

Miss Pitt bangs the gong. The kids have a big hit!

Teacher/Parent Pages

Use the following questions to stimulate language growth, imagination, conceptual relationships, and higher-level thinking skills. These activities will encourage conversation and help develop language skills. Students must know that their ideas are important and that their questions will be heard. Have fun and accept all reasonable answers while praising and encouraging questioning from the students.

Vocabulary Expansion

Describe and define these words and phrases:

talent show	bang a gong	a big hit
put on	different	tap dancing
select a winner	performance	can't miss
act	excellent	dig it
perform well	talented	saxophone

Language Expansion Activities

1. Plan a talent show for your group. Decide what each person could do best. Make a program for your talent show. List all the performers and the titles of their acts.

2. Learn a poem. After you memorize it, say it for the students in your group.

Language Expansion Questions

1. Why have the kids' families all gathered together?

2. What was meant by the following: "The kids can sing, tap, kick, hiss, and zap"?

3. What was Kim's special talent? Did the others enjoy it? Explain why you think so.

4. Who are the two tap dancers? What do you think they had to do before the talent show?

5. What kind of act did Sam and Sid do? What do you think really happened to Sam?

6. In this story, what instrument did Nick play? What kind of music did he play?

7. Different people enjoy different types of entertainment. What is your favorite kind of show? Write about it.

8. Imagine some kind of entertainment that you have never had a chance to see in person, but would like to. Why might it be more exciting in person than on TV?

9. People watch TV to be entertained. What kinds of things do you think people did before they had TV?

10. At your home, what things do people enjoy doing together? What things would you like to do more often? Why?

Unit 11, Book 1

AL'S WISH

UNIT 11

Phonology/Orthography Concepts

- The consonant letter (grapheme) pairs **sh**, **th**, **ch**, and **wh** combine to create a single sound (phoneme).
  - /*th*/ may be a voiced (this, that, them) or voiceless (thin, think, thick) phoneme.
- **Letter pairs** that create a single sound (phoneme) are called **digraphs**.

Vocabulary

bath	rich	thin	*are*
cash	shack	thing	*put*
chap	shall	think	
chat	ships	this	
chill	shock	wham	
chip	shop	which	
dash	shot	whiff	
dish	than	wish	
fish	thank	with	
math	that		
pinch	thick		

AL'S WISH

Story Summary:

Al is at his computer playing his favorite game, *Rats on Hills*. He wishes he were at the beach, and he begins to daydream. He imagines that he sees one of the rats from the game lying in a hammock on the beach. He tries to be friendly, but the mean rat grabs Al's snack. Al punches the rat. The rat runs off and Al takes his place in the hammock.

Al is at his PC. Al can put *Rats on Hills* in the PC. Al nods off. What will Al think of? Al has a wish.

Al's wish was to sit with a rat and chat. Which of the six rats was this?

Al was in shock. It was Rat Six, the rich king rat.

Al hits it off with Rat Six. Al pats him with tan mix.

Al fans Rat Six with his big, thin fan.

Rat said to Al, "Al, you shot the six rats on the six hills to have a big win. The rats did

not wish you to win on the hills. The rats are mad."

Al sits and thinks. Al has thick fish and thin chips. Rat gets a whiff of the fish and chips.

Rat rips off Al's fish and chips. Rat Six robs Al. Al is mad at the king rat.

Al said, "You can not rip off the fish and chips. I am mad!" Wham! Al jabs Rat Six!

Rat Six runs off with a shock. Rat Six is not the king rat. "Dash off. Rat Six," Al said.

Al pops in to the king rat's net. Al sips a can of pop and thinks, "I can pass Rat Six on his six hills. I can do it. I am the king rat!"

Teacher/Parent Pages

Use the following questions to stimulate language growth, imagination, conceptual relationships, and higher-level thinking skills. These activities will encourage conversation and help develop language skills. Students must know that their ideas are important and that their questions will be heard. Have fun and accept all reasonable answers while praising and encouraging questioning from the students.

Vocabulary Expansion

Describe and define these words and phrases:

daydream	far-fetched	had enough
fantasy	vacationing	coward
imagination	beach	approach
make-believe	hammock	imagine
mind	suntan oil	pinch

Language Expansion Activities

1. Make up another version of the *Rats on Hills* computer game. Tell how to play it.

2. Pretend you are dreaming. Draw a picture of something that you are dreaming. Write a story to go along with the picture.

Language Expansion Questions

1. What game was Al playing on the computer before he started to daydream?

2. Who did Al meet in his dream?

3. Al wanted to be friends with Rat Six. What did he do to show his friendship?

4. How did Rat Six treat Al?

5. Al got very angry with Rat Six and punched him. What happened to Rat Six?

6. At the end of the story, was Al still dreaming? How do you know?

7. Have you ever had a daydream? What happened in your dream? Was your dream better or worse than Al's?

8. Change the story so that Al and Rat Six became friends on the beach. Write the new story.

9. This story was a fantasy. Are there any parts of the story that could really happen?

10. Al's dream took place on the beach. If you were to have a very good dream, where would you want it to take place? Why?

THIN THAD

UNIT 11

Phonology/Orthography Concepts

- The consonant letter (grapheme) pairs **sh**, **th**, **ch**, and **wh** combine to create a single sound (phoneme).
  - /*th*/ may be a voiced (this, that, them) or voiceless (thin, think, thick) phoneme.

- **Letter pairs** that create a single sound (phoneme) are called **digraphs**.

Vocabulary

bath	rich	thin	*are*
cash	shack	thing	*put*
chap	shall	think	
chat	ships	this	
chill	shock	wham	
chip	shop	which	
dash	shot	whiff	
dish	than	wish	
fish	thank	with	
math	that		
pinch	thick		

THIN THAD

Story Summary:

Thin Thad is the school custodian. He repairs all kinds of things, and the children and teachers all like him because he is so thoughtful. One day, Miss Pitt notices an odor of gas and she sends Sid to get Thin Thad. Thad instructs Miss Pitt and the children to vacate the room while he repairs the gas tank. Later, the children go to recess and entice Thin Thad to join in their softball game.

Thin Thad is the chap that can fix things. The kids think Thad is rad. He has a shop with kits, sacks, rags, fans, pads, lids, mops, bats, and pans.

Sid ran to Thin Thad. "Thad! Thad! I was in math. Miss Pitt got a whiff of gas. Miss Pitt thinks that chips are in the gas tank!"

Thad puts his things in his shop kit. Thad thinks, "I shall dash to fix the gas tank."

 "Miss Pitt, you will have to dash off with the kids till I fix the tank," said Thad.

Thin Thad thinks, "Which tank is shot?" Thad got a whiff of gas and said, "This is the tank which I will fix."

"Thank you, thank you," said Miss Pitt to Thad. The kids said, "Thank you, Thad."

Thad put his things back in his shop kit. Thad got back to his shop. _____

Ring! Ring! The kids dash off. "I have the mitts," said Sam.

"Have you got the bats?" said Sid.

Sam said, "The bats and pads are in Thad's shop."

"Thad, can I have the bats and pads?" said Sid. Thad got the things for Sid. "Thad, can you bat with the gang?" said Sid.

Thad puts the bats and pads in a thick bag. Thad and Sid dash back to the gang.

Sam is at bat. Wham! Sam has a hit. Sid can not hit. Thad will pinch hit.

Thad is at bat. Wham! Bam! Thin Thad can hit it to the rim! Thad can dash. Thad has a big win!

Teacher/Parent Pages

Use the following questions to stimulate language growth, imagination, conceptual relationships, and higher-level thinking skills. These activities will encourage conversation and help develop language skills. Students must know that their ideas are important and that their questions will be heard. Have fun and accept all reasonable answers while praising and encouraging questioning from the students.

Vocabulary Expansion

Describe and define these words and phrases:

vacate
custodian
maintenance
school supplies
equipment

sports
recess
emergency
odor
notice
instruct

repair
join in
locker
bases
thoughtful

Language Expansion Activities

1. With clay, make a ball field. Mold figures of Sam and Sid in the outfield. Mold a figure of Thin Thad at bat. Mold little balls, mitts, and bats. Tell the story using the figures you created.

2. Pretend you are the school custodian. What jobs would you do during the day?

Language Expansion Questions

1. Who is Thin Thad?

2. How does Thad help Miss Pitt and the children in the math class? Think of two ways Thad helped people in this story.

3. Sam gets a turn at bat. What happens when Thad bats?

4. Do you think Thin Thad likes his job? Why is a job like Thad's a good one to have?

5. Do you think the children in this school like Thin Thad? How do you know?

6. Thin Thad has many jobs during the school day. Try to think of as many of his jobs as you can.

7. People have different jobs when they grow up. What kind of job would you like to have? If you had that job, what kind of work would you do every day?

8. Do you think that it would be important to have a job that you really like to do? Why?

9. In Thin Thad's job, he helps people. What other kinds of jobs help people?

10. Some people like their jobs. But some people don't like their jobs. Do you think that sometimes people have to do jobs that they don't really like? What jobs around the house do you have? Do you like all of them? Do they have to be done?

CHICK'S FISH SHACK

UNIT 11

Phonology/Orthography Concepts

- The consonant letter (grapheme) pairs **sh**, **th**, **ch**, and **wh** combine to create a single sound (phoneme).
  - /*th*/ may be a voiced (this, that, them) or voiceless (thin, think, thick) phoneme.

- **Letter pairs** that create a single sound (phoneme) are called **digraphs**.

Vocabulary

bath	rich	thin	*are*
cash	shack	thing	*put*
chap	shall	think	
chat	ships	this	
chill	shock	wham	
chip	shop	which	
dash	shot	whiff	
dish	than	wish	
fish	thank	with	
math	that		
pinch	thick		

CHICK'S FISH SHACK

Story Summary:

Mat's dad has opened a fish shop down at the dock. Huge boats and ships come into the harbor, and he purchases his fish from the captains. Mat assists his dad in the store after school and on weekends. Many people buy fish from Chick. One evening, when Pam gets off work, she stops by to buy some fish and chips from Chick. Pam and Chick are both adults who are lonely, and they become friends.

Mat's dad is Chick. Chick has a fish shop. It is Chick's Fish Shack. Chick's Fish Shack is at the dock. Lots of big ships are at the dock.

The ships have lots of fish, and Chick shops on the ships. Chick's job is to fill the sacks

with fish and put the fish in a thick tin box to chill it.

Mat's job is to put the fish in thick bags. Moms and dads are at the fish shack for the bags of fish.

Which fish has Sam's dad got in his bag? It is a thin cod fish.

Sid's mom has cash to shop. "I have a thick rich bass, if you wish," said Chick.

"I will have the bass," said Sid's mom.

Chick locks the cash in his big cash box.

Sid's mom puts the fish in the van. Sid's mom has to dash back to a job.

Pam got off at six. "What can I fix?" Pam said. "I will fix fish and chips." Pam locks the shop.

Pam ran to Chick's Fish Shack. "Is Mat at the shop?" Pam said to Chick.

"Mat is not at the shop," said Chick. "Mat's gang is at the rink."

"I think I will have fish and chips. Can you put fish and chips in a sack?" said Pam.

"I shall," said Chick.

Pam thinks Chick is tops.

Chick thinks, "Pam is a doll. I wish Mat had a mom."

Teacher/Parent Pages

Use the following questions to stimulate language growth, imagination, conceptual relationships, and higher-level thinking skills. These activities will encourage conversation and help develop language skills. Students must know that their ideas are important and that their questions will be heard. Have fun and accept all reasonable answers while praising and encouraging questioning from the students.

Vocabulary Expansion

Describe and define these words and phrases:

assist	purchase	wishful thinking
weekend	cash register	cash
harbor	adults	ships
dock	lonely	mall
captains	chips	cooler

Language Expansion Activities

1. Pretend you are the owner of a fish shop. Have the kids in the class come in and order fish to go. Wrap it up and take the money.

2. Draw a picture of a dock with stores and boats and beaches.

Language Expansion Questions

1. What was the name of Mat's dad's store?

2. What did Chick sell?

3. Where did Chick go to get the fish? Do you think it was fresh fish? Why?

4. What kinds of things did Mat do to help his dad? List them.

5. Pam, the lady who owns Pam's Lunch Hut, went to Chick's for fresh fish. What did she and Chick talk about? Do you think they liked each other? Why?

6. Have you ever been to a fish shop? What does it smell like? What kinds of things did you buy?

7. Mat had to help his dad in the shop. Do you ever have to help your parents where they work or at home? What kinds of things do you do? Write a story about how you help.

8. Sometimes Mat wants to go out and play instead of helping in the shop. How do you think you would feel if you had to work every day?

9. Do you think this story is fact or fantasy? Why?

10. The fish shop is at the dock. Have you ever been to a dock? What kinds of things did you see and do there?

JEN WELLS'S PET SHOP

UNIT 12

Phonology/Orthography Concepts

- A single unit of sound is a phoneme.
  - Vowel phonemes are open sounds.
  - Consonant sounds are closed sounds.
  - Combined sounds create words we hear.
- Letters are symbols (graphemes) that represent vowel or consonant sounds.
  - Combined letters create words we write and read.
- Vowel sound-symbol relationship: short /e/

Vocabulary

bed	less	shell	when
beg	let	Ted	wet
bell	men	tell	yet
Bell	mess	ten	
bet	met	them	
chess	Nell	then	*should*
fell	nets	vet	*would*
get	pen	yell	*could*
Jen	pet	yes	
Ken	red	yet	
led	sell	well	
leg	set	Wells	

JEN WELLS'S PET SHOP

Story Summary:

Jen Wells owns the pet shop at the dock. Jen is a friend of Miss Pitt's. There are many animals in the shop and sometimes things get out of hand. One afternoon, Nell Pitt drops by. Jen tells her about the ten Labrador puppies that escaped and almost drowned. Later, Ted comes in the shop and buys a cat to keep rats out of his shell shop.

 Miss Jen Wells has a big pet shop. Miss Wells's pet shop was at the dock with Chick's Fish Shack and Ted's Shell Shop.

Nell Pitt and Jen Wells were pals. When Nell would get to Jen's pet shop, Nell would yell, "Jen! Jen!"

Jen's pets could have a big mess in the shop. When the bell rang and Jen fed the pets, the cats would yip and yap and dash to the dish of fish.

When Jen rang the big bell, the dogs would dash to the big red dish and whiff the thick rich chops that Jen put in the dish.

"Jen, did you tell Nell of the ten wet labs that are at the vet's?" said Ted, an odd man that ran Ted's Shell Shop.

"Yes," Jen said. "Ted and Pam could tell you, Nell. The labs ran off to the ships as quick as a shot. The dogs fell in and got wet. Thanks to Ted and Pam, and to the men on the ships, I got them back and to the vet's."

Ted said, "What I think I should have is a cat for a pet at the shell shop. A cat would kill the rats on the dock. I can not have rats in the shell shop."

"I think you should," Jen said.

"Well," said Nell, "if you sell Ted the big black cat, you should sell him a cat bed for it as well."

Ted got the black cat and the cat bed and when Ted got back to his shell shop, put them in the back.

Ring! Ring! The bell rings. It is the vet to tell Jen that the ten wet labs are well.

Jen and Nell dash off in Jen's big red pet van to get the labs.

When Jen and Nell get to the vet's, Jen honks and the vet puts the labs in the back for them. "Thank you," said Jen to the vet. "I am off to the pet shop."

Teacher/Parent Pages

Use the following questions to stimulate language growth, imagination, conceptual relationships, and higher-level thinking skills. These activities will encourage conversation and help develop language skills. Students must know that their ideas are important and that their questions will be heard. Have fun and accept all reasonable answers while praising and encouraging questioning from the students.

Vocabulary Expansion

Describe and define these words and phrases:

owned	occurred	puppies
out of hand	labs	quick as a shot
drop by	rescue	Labrador Retriever
dramatic	shells	pet shop
event	pick up	shell shop

Language Expansion Activities

1. Jen Wells had lots of pets in her shop. Draw a picture of the pet shop and explain what kinds of things have to be done for different kinds of pets.

2. Visit a veterinarian's office, or invite a vet to come to your class. Then make a group report about all of the work veterinarians do.

Language Expansion Questions

1. Who was Jen Wells' good friend?

2. What happened when Jen fed the pets?

3. Tell the story that Ted and Jen told Miss Nell Pitt.

4. What kind of pet did Ted need? Why?

5. Explain what the men on the dock did to help Jen get the ten puppies back. Do people always help each other? Why?

6. Describe how you feel when you help another person or an animal. Write a story about those feelings.

7. Adults can have many kinds of jobs. What jobs involve helping people? What jobs involve helping animals?

8. Do you know a pet that has been in an accident? Tell about it.

9. Pet shops have pets for sale. What other things can be sold in pet shops?

10. When you have a friend, you enjoy doing things for him or her. Miss Pitt helped Jen Wells. What have you done to help your friends?

TED'S SHELL SHOP

UNIT 12

Phonology/Orthography Concepts

- A single unit of sound is a phoneme.
  - Vowel phonemes are open sounds.
  - Consonant sounds are closed sounds.
  - Combined sounds create words we hear.
- Letters are symbols (graphemes) that represent vowel or consonant sounds.
  - Combined letters create words we write and read.
- Vowel sound-symbol relationship: short /e/

Vocabulary

bed	less	shell	when
beg	let	Ted	wet
bell	men	tell	yet
Bell	mess	ten	
bet	met	them	
chess	Nell	then	*should*
fell	nets	vet	*would*
get	pen	yell	*could*
Jen	pet	yes	
Ken	red	yet	
led	sell	well	
leg	set	Wells	

TED'S SHELL SHOP

Story Summary:

Ted is an old sailor with a peg leg. He owns a little shell shop at the dock. Ted loves kids and often tells them sea stories and gives them shells. Ken Bell, the boys' scout leader, arrives at the dock with his scout troop. The boys are going to sleep over on a ship. Ted wishes them good luck as they leave.

 Ted's Shell Shop is at the dock. Ted is an odd chap. He has a peg leg. Ted gets shells from men on the big ships.

The men get the shells in big, thick nets which the men toss from the big ships.

When Ted was a lad, he went for shells, and his ship sank. Ted fell in and got his bad leg.

 Ted led lots of ships. Ted could fix the big ships at the dock.

When the kids met at the dock, Ted would tell them of the big, long ships. Ted would not yell at the kids. He would let them pet his cats and put shells on the shelf.

Tam is at the dock with Sis, Bill, and Jill.

Sis thinks, "I wish I could have that big, pink, conch shell."

Ted said, "I have tan shells, Sis. The tan shells are not as big as the pink conch shells. Yet the tan shells have big red dots."

"I could let you have a tan shell with red dots. When shells have chips in them, I can not sell them. I have a tan shell that has a chip. I will get it for you, Sis."

"Thank you! Thank you, Ted," said Sis. "I will put this tan shell on the top shelf in the den."

Ted said, "Tam, Bill and Jill should not bat at the black cat. The cat will dash off and chip the shells." Ted got a pop for Bill and Jill.

"Thank you, Ted," said Tam, "I will not let them bat the cat."

Sam, Sid, Al , Nick, and Ken Bell met Tam and Ted. The kids had mess kits with them. "The lads and I will get on the long ship at six," said Ken Bell. "I think you could tell them of trips on the long ships when you were a lad, Ted. The lads and I wish that you could get on the ship with us."

Mat met Ken and the lads. Mat had his mess kit and his back pack.

Ted said, "I will think of you when you are on the ship! You chaps can tell of the long ship when you get back to the dock."

Teacher/Parent Pages

Use the following questions to stimulate language growth, imagination, conceptual relationships, and higher-level thinking skills. These activities will encourage conversation and help develop language skills. Students must know that their ideas are important and that their questions will be heard. Have fun and accept all reasonable answers while praising and encouraging questioning from the students.

Vocabulary Expansion

Describe and define these words and phrases:

operate	bon voyage	scout leader
result	sailor	tall ships
accident	stroller	the sea
window shop	twins	peg leg
overnight	scouts	sell

Language Expansion Activities

1. Bring shells to class. Put them in groups according to size and color. Ask the librarian to help you find a book on shells, and then make a label for each shell.

2. Tell about a special trip you have taken or a special adventure you have had.

Language Expansion Questions

1. What was sold in Ted's store at the dock?

2. What was unusual about Ted's appearance? Ted could have chosen a more up-to-date prosthetic in exchange for his peg leg. Many people have artificial limbs that allow them to dance, skate, and ride bikes as well as anybody else. Why do you think Ted decided not to use a modern prosthetic?

3. Write a story about the accident Ted had when he was a young man.

4. What was said in the story to make you think the kids really liked Ted?

5. Describe the special shell that Sis wanted. Have you ever held a conch shell? What is unusual about it?

6. Describe the special shell that Ted gave Sis.

7. Some adults enjoy giving gifts to children. Can you remember a gift you have received from an adult? Why did that person like you well enough to give you a special gift?

8. Why were the boys all meeting at the dock? Why did they want Ted to go with them?

9. Ted had a handicap. What does that mean? What other kinds of handicaps do people have? Sometimes people are cruel to handicapped people and call them names like "peg leg." Why do you think some people do that? What can others do to prevent these horrible comments?

10. Tell about all the things the boys might do on the long ship. What would be the most fun for you?

KEN BELL

UNIT 12

Phonology/Orthography Concepts

- A single unit of sound is a phoneme.
  - Vowel phonemes are open sounds.
  - Consonant sounds are closed sounds.
  - Combined sounds create words we hear.
- Letters are symbols (graphemes) that represent vowel or consonant sounds.
  - Combined letters create words we write and read.
- Vowel sound-symbol relationship: short /e/

Vocabulary

bed	less	shell	when
beg	let	Ted	wet
bell	men	tell	yet
Bell	mess	ten	
bet	met	them	
chess	Nell	then	*should*
fell	nets	vet	*would*
get	pen	yell	*could*
Jen	pet	yes	
Ken	red	yet	
led	sell	well	
leg	set	Wells	

KEN BELL

Story Summary:

Scout leader Ken Bell takes the boys aboard a tall ship for an overnight sea adventure. The boys meet at the dock with their gear. After Ken's instructions, they board the ship. Sid, who isn't listening very well, falls in and gets himself and all his gear wet. Ken is firm but gentle with Sid. Then the boys set sail. A long day of fishing and working the nets leaves the young boys tired and hungry. They hurry to the mess hall telling their own tall tales. Ken Bell's adventure is a success!

Ken Bell led Sam, Sid, Al, Nick, and Mat to the long ship. When his den met, Ken would yell, "Get set!" Ken led them well.

Ken would get them the mess kits and back packs with beds.
When they would beg him, Ken would let them have his chess set.

When the lads got on the ship, Ken would not let them get the kegs and nets wet.

The kids fed the ship's cats fish, and Ken set the mess kits and back packs in the ship's big pen.

When Ken got them on the ship, Sid fell off and got his back, bed, and mess kit wet.

Ken and the men got Sid back on the ship.

"Sit on the cot and let me get you the big red bath mat."

Ken did not yell at Sid. Ken said, "Sid, sit till you are not wet."

Sid sits and thinks, "I will have to thank Ken. When I fell in, Ken did not yell. Ken got me the red mat. Ken is tops!"

When the men let the lads set the nets to fish, Sam and Nick get a whiff of the shell fish and wish for the mess bell to ring.

The lads get ten red bass. It is a rich net!

Ring! Ring! The big red mess bell rings and the men and lads dash to the back of the ship.

The lads tell of fish nets, bass, shells, kegs, ship's cats, and a wet Sid. The ship is a hit with the kids.

When the lads set off to bed, the lads thank Ken and the ship's men.

Teacher/Parent Pages

Use the following questions to stimulate language growth, imagination, conceptual relationships, and higher-level thinking skills. These activities will encourage conversation and help develop language skills. Students must know that their ideas are important and that their questions will be heard. Have fun and accept all reasonable answers while praising and encouraging questioning from the students.

Vocabulary Expansion

Describe and define these words and phrases:

get set	set sail	relieved
scout den	tall ship	tall tales
beg	adventure	bass
chess set	listen	fish nets
mess kits	dry off	success

Language Expansion Activities

1. Sailors tell tall tales. Create a tall tale of your own. Write it down, draw one or two illustrations to go with it, and share it with your group.

2. When people are not careful, accidents happen. Make a list of safety rules and post them in your classroom.

Language Expansion Questions

1. Who was the scout leader? What was the special trip the boys were having?

2. Ken had something special that the boys liked to play a game with. What was it? Have you ever seen one?

3. What kinds of things might you be able to do aboard a ship to amuse yourself?

4. What special kinds of jobs and responsibilities are necessary aboard a ship? List them.

5. Explain what happened to Sid. Why did he think, "I will have to thank Ken"?

6. How is fishing with nets different from fishing with poles? With rods and reels? Ask someone who has been fishing to tell about it.

7. What does "mess" mean in this story? What do you think a mess hall is?

8. The men caught shellfish. How are shellfish different from other fish? Describe the way they looked.

9. Imagine what kinds of things the ship's men might have shown the boys. What new things could they have learned to do?

10. If you were the captain of a tall ship, where would you like to sail? Try to find a picture of the place and describe it to your friends.